Ma'khai The Magnificent

Young Buddha Press

Ma'khai The Magnificent by Kasheera Hickson and Mark Savage Jr.
Published by Young Buddha Press Los Angeles, Ca 91405

www.YoungBuddhaPress.com

Printed in the United States of America

First Printing, 2018

For information about special discounts available for bulk purchases, sales
promotions, fund-raising and educational needs, contact Young Buddha Press
Company Sales at 1-707-276-6334 or info@youngbuddhapress.com.

Library of Congress Control Number: 2018914449

ISBN: 978-0-9990678-2-6

10 9 8 7 6 5 4 3 2 1

Hi, My name is Ma'khai.
Ma'khai The Magnificent!

I can draw a masterpiece.

I can brighten up the day.

1 2 3 4 5 6 7 8 9 10 11 12...100

I can count 1 to 100.

I can go outside and play.

I can do anything, I'm Magnificent!

I can sing the ABC's.

I can jump into the air.

I can dance to the music.

I can learn how to share.

I can do
anything,
I'm
Magnificent!

I can give a kiss and hug.

I can help clean up the house.

I can speak very loudly,

or as quiet as a mouse.

I can do anything,
I'm
Magnificent!

I can climb the highest mountain.

I can journey really far.

I can practice mindfulness.

I can marvel at the stars.

I can do anything, I'm Magnificent!

I can live in the moment.

SUCCESS
FOR
TODDLERS

BY
WATKHATSATASE

I can learn how to lead.

I can be a light that shines.

I'm determined to succeed!

I can do
so many things
because I am
Magnificent
and
YOU ARE TOO!

www.ingramcontent.com/pod-product-compliance
Lightning Source LLC
Chambersburg PA
CBHW040251100426

42811CB00011B/1228